Copycat Cooking
for Beginners

How to leave your family and friends speechless by recreating these famous restaurant recipes.

William Oliver Thomas & Ernest D.W

Table of Content

INTRODUCTION 6

BENEFITS OF COOKING AT HOME 8

PRACTICAL ADVICE FOR BEGINNERS ON THE CORRECT DISTRIBUTION OF MEALS DURING THE DAY, TO DIGEST WELL AND AVOID GAINING WEIGHT 14

ENERGIZING SMOOTHIE & MILK SHAKE RECIPES 18

PEACH PERFECTION SMOOTHIE..19
STRAWBERRY RASPBERRY BANANA SMOOTHIE...20
MANGO-A-GO-GO SMOOTHIE...21
JAMBA JUICE: PROTEIN BERRY WORKOUT.......................................23
HOMEMADE STRAWBERRY-MANGO SMOOTHIE...............................24
JAMBA JUICE: STRAWBERRY SURF RIDER.......................................25
PANERA BREAD: PEACH & BLUEBERRY SMOOTHIE 27
PANERA'S COPYCAT MANGO SMOOTHIE 29
NAKED JUICE: GREEN MACHINE SMOOTHIE 30
NAKED JUICE: RED MACHINE 31
COOKIES & CREAM SHAKE 32
MCDONALD'S COPYCAT SHAMROCK SHAKE 33
WENDY'S COPYCAT CHOCOLATE FROSTY 35
JACK IN THE BOX'S COPYCAT PUMPKIN PIE SHAKE..........................36
CHERRY & VANILLA SHAKE...37

SOUP RECIPES...38

PF CHANG'S HOT AND SOUR SOUP 39
DISNEYLAND'S MONTEREY CLAM CHOWDER 41
OUTBACK'S BAKED POTATO SOUP...43
APPLEBEE'S TOMATO BASIL SOUP 46

RECIPES FOR BREAD 47

RED ROBIN BURGER 48
SAUTÉED MUSHROOM BURGER 50
WHISKY RIVER BURGER...51
TUSCAN BUTTER BURGER 52
FOUR CHEESE MELT 55
THE BOSS BURGER 57
ALEX'S SANTA FE BURGER 58
....59

The Southern Charm Burger... 60

Chili's Avocado Beef Burger 63

Tuna Salad Wraps 65

Ranchero Chicken Tacos 67

Mushroom Jack Chicken Fajitas 69

Greek Chicken Wraps 73

Chicken Quesadillas... 75

SWEET AND SAVORY SNACK RECIPES...**77**

Low Fat Veggie Quesadilla.. 78

Garlic Mashed Potatoes 81

Vegetable Medley 82

Big Ol' Brownie 85

Lasagna with Feta and Black Olives 86

Easy Copycat Monterey's Little Mexico Queso 87

Fried Keto Cheese with Mushrooms 89

Mushroom Recipe Stuffed with Cheese, Spinach, and Bacon 90

DESSERT AND PASTRY RECIPES **92**

Campfire S'mores... 93

Banana Pudding 95

Starbuck's Copycat Cranberry Chocolate Bliss Bars 97

Chili's New York Style Cheesecake 98

Chocolate Pecan Pie 100

Peanut Butter Kisses 102

Cornbread Muffins 104

Chocolate Mousse Cake.. 105

Blackberry and Apples Cobbler 107

DELICIOUS IDEAS FOR KIDS **108**

PRACTICAL ADVICE FOR BEGINNERS TO CANNING AND PRESERVING YOUR FAVORITE FOODS **112**

CONCLUSION...**118**

WHERE ARE YOUR SWEETHEART RECIPES? **120**

Introduction

Dear Reader,

My name is William Oliver Thomas. I am an experienced chef with a passion for good food. With this book, I want to show you that you don't need a spell to prepare nutritious and delicious meals that taste just like those at famous restaurants.

In the following chapters, we'll first discuss the benefits of cooking at home. Then I'll give you practical tips for beginners on proper meal planning, digesting well, and avoiding gaining weight.

To start your meal, you could have a tasteful soup or light appetizer as a main course and then finish with a tasty main course.

If you like to have a light snack in the early afternoon, you will also find information in this book to learn how to prepare them easily.
In the evening, after a good dinner, you could end your day with a mouth-watering dessert or a cake made with your own hands that will help you stay in a good mood.
Homemade cakes and sweets are better and more genuine than those we buy.
They are cakes that we make ourselves, as we want them, and with ingredients that we choose. Also cooking at home allows us to save a lot of money.

Do you want to offer your guests or your family something special? With this book, you will have the opportunity to find and create many new recipes. Enrich your creations with the most imaginative decorations, enjoy the aroma and smell of food, Snacks, and desserts made in the comfort of your kitchen!

In this book, you will find many recipes divided into different categories to enrich your dishes and enjoy every meal as a moment of full enjoyment! You'll be able to combine them with other recipes you've received from friends and family or with recipes you may have already tried in other restaurants.

Imagine hearing the sound of water boiling in the background as you cut fresh, crisp vegetables. Smell the intense aroma of spices and herbs as you mix sauces and condiments. Imagine the joy of your guests as they prepare for a delicious meal you are cooking for them.

Imagine the explosion of your taste buds as you enjoy the final flavor of your creations, accentuated by the satisfaction of having cooked and created everything yourself.

PS.
When I first learned to cook, I would randomly jot down the changes I made to the ingredients next to the dishes. I fold the corners of the pages to find my favorite recipes faster. My cookbooks were not pretty to look that.
While writing this book, I decided to include a space for notes next to each recipe. You'll find a tab at the end of the book where you can note which page your favorite recipes are on.

Benefits of Cooking at Home

Meals in the restaurant can contain several unhealthy ingredients. There is also much more than what you lack when you feed on a take-outs. These are some explanations of why you should consider having your cooking dinner tonight!

A Nutrient-Dense Plate

If prepared food arrives from outside the home, you typically have limited knowledge about salt, sugar, and processed oils. For a fact, we also apply more to our meal when it is served to the table. You will say how much salt, sugar, and oil are being used to prepare meals at home.

Increased Fruit and Vegetable Intake

The typical western diet loses both the weight and durability of plant foods we need to preserve. Many People eat only two fresh fruit and vegetables a day, while at least five portions are required. Tons of premade food, like restaurant food goods, restrict fruit and vegetable parts. By supplying you with the convenience of cooking at home, you have complete control over your food. The message to note is that your attention will continue with the intake of more fruit and vegetables. Attach them to your cooking, snack them, or exchange them with your relatives on their way. Then take steps towards organic alternatives. It is always better to eat entire fruits and vegetables, whether or not organic, than processed foods.

Save Money and Use What You Have

Just because you haven't visited your local health food or food store this week doesn't mean you get stuck with taking in. Open your cupboard and fridge and see what you can make for a meal. It can be as easy as gluten-free rice, roasted tomatoes, carrots, frozen vegetables, and lemon juice. This simple meal is packed with fiber, protein, vitamins, and minerals. Best of all, in less than 30 minutes, it is delicious and can be prepared. You can save up your money in the long run and allows you sufficient food to share with or break the next day.

Sensible Snacking

Bringing premade snacks saves time, but everything goes back to what's in these products still. Don't worry, you can still have your guilty pleasures, but there is a way to make them more nutritious and often taste better. Swap your chips and dip the chopped vegetables into hummus. Create your snacks with bagged potato chips or carrots. Take a bowl and make your popcorn on top of your stove or in the popcorn machine. You can manage the amount of salt, sugar, and oil added.

Share Your Delicious Health

Once you make your recipes, you are so proud of your achievements. Furthermore, the food tastes amazing. Don't confuse me now—some of your inventive recipes won't taste the same thing, but friends and family will love your cuisine with constant practice and experimentation. You will see them enjoy the best nutritious food because of you and your faith in spreading health and love.

It Gives You a Chance to Reconnect

Having that chance to cook together helps you reconnect with your partner and your loved ones. Cooking also has other benefits. The American Psychological Association says that working together with new things—like learning a new recipe—can help maintain a relationship.

It's Proven to Be Healthier

Many researchers say that those who eat more often than not have a healthier diet overall. Such studies also show that in restaurants, menus, salt, saturated fat, total fat, and average calories are typically higher than in-house diets.
You have complete control over your food, whether you put fresh products together or shipped them straight to your door using a company like Plated. It can make a difference in your overall health.

It's Easier to Watch Your Calories

The average fast-food order is between 1,100 and 1,200 calories in total–nearly all the highly recommended daily calorie intake is 1,600 to 2,400 calories by a woman and almost two thirds (2,000 to 3,000 calories) a man daily. So, think again if you felt the independent restaurants so smaller chains would do well. Such products suck up an average of 1.327 calories per meal of additional calories.

Adult BMI Calculation Formula

$$\text{BMI} = \frac{\text{(your weight in pounds)} \ X \ 703}{\text{(your height in inches)}^2}$$

FOR EXAMPLE:
If you weigh **120 pounds** and are **5 ft. 3in** (63in.) tall:

$$\text{BMI} = \frac{120 \ X \ 703}{63^2} = \frac{84,360}{3,969} = 21.3$$

This is well within the healthy weight range

Creating your food ensures you can guarantee that the portion sizes and calories are where you want them. Recipes also come with nutritional information and tips for sizing, which ease this.

Body Mass Index Interpretation

BMI < 18.5: Below normal weight
BMI >= 18.5 and < 25: Normal weight
BMI >= 25 and < 30: Overweight
BMI >= 30 and < 35: Class I Obesity
BMI >= 35 and < 40: Class II Obesity
BMI >= 40: Class III Obesity

It's a Time Saver

Part of shopping is to wait for food to come or travel to get it. It may take much more time, depending on where you live, what time you order, and whether or not the delivery person is good at directions!

It doesn't have to take much time to cook at home if you don't want it. You remove the need to search for ingredients or foodstuffs by using a service like Plated. Everything you need is at your house, in the exact amount that you use.

It can be a money saver, too

In the long run, home-cooked food will save you money. A collection of basic ingredients also arrive at a lower price than a single dish. You can also consume more of a meal at home than if you buy a take-out or rest to work the next day. After a few weeks, you will see big savings starting to add up

It's Personalized

Cooking at home gives you the chance to enjoy the food you want, how you like it. For starters, with Plated, if you want your meat more well-done or less sweet, the formula includes suggested changes.

Cutting Costs

Nobody has to remind you that it's pricey to eat out. The disparity between a local restaurant sandwich and a kitchen sandwich is more than a feeling. The purchasing of packaged food in a restaurant typically costs far more than the buying of your

products. Cooking at home helps you get more for your money by raising the excess expenses of cooking and servicing restaurants. The more often you make your food, the more money you save.

Enjoying the Process

Once you come back home from a busy day, there is little more enjoyable than disconnecting from work emails, voicemails, unfinished assignments, or homework. Cooking at home presents you with a break from your routine and space for imagination. Rather than listen to noisy messages, you should put on the radio, collect spices, and reflect on the sizzle's odors on the stove or roast vegetables. It may stun you on how much you might like it when you make a daily habit of preparing food.

If your breakfast is great, lunch soup, or fresh tomato sauce for dinner, home cooking is a worthy investment. In return for your time and energy in preparation, you will benefit richly— from cost savings to fun with friends.

And the more you enjoy cooking in the kitchen, the more you get to make fantastic food!

Try Plated

Ready to download and cook your smartphone? Plated is a kind of a meal kit delivery service that offers all the above and more positive features! Choose from a weekly menu of designed recipes and get all you need right at your door. Pre-portioned foods are of the highest quality only and contain fresh, seasonal, organically, and sustainable seafood items and hormone-free meat.
Recipes vary from meals that require just 30 minutes to prepare, which is as demanding as its rewards. Where people find dinner a delight to consume and cook.

Practical Advice for Beginners on the Correct Distribution of Meals During the Day, to Digest Well and Avoid Gaining Weight

Shifting to a healthy lifestyle seems to be intimidating. Being committed to your preferred diet, slowly and reasonably, will provide you lifelong changes and optimum health.

Start by selecting what seems doable to you. Follow your instincts when something piques your interest. You are the best at knowing what's right for you and what you will or will not eat or drink.

Be willing to trying something new because you will have to do something different, on purpose, if you want a different result. Don't worry about what you might give up. You don't have to decide to give up anything right now. Keep it easy. Once you go through the benefits of feeling better, having more energy, and looking better, it will be easier to embrace and maintain a healthy eating lifestyle.

The effortless mistake we've made by just only eating our food makes it a significant difference. It is vital to think that when it comes to our meals, timing is the key.

As for your breakfast, eating within 30 minutes of waking up is essential. 7 in the morning is the best time to have breakfast. Make sure to have your meal no later than 10 a.m. and always have protein in your breakfast.

Lastly, at 7 p.m., dinner is the perfect time to have your meal. It would be perfect for you to keep a 3 hours gap between dinner and bedtime. Have your meal before 10 p.m. because eating dinner close to bedtime might affect your good night's sleep.

One way to adapt a healthy eating lifestyle is to add vegetables and fruit to what you already eat gradually.
• At breakfast, include bananas, blueberries, blackberries, strawberries, or raspberries. Add spinach, onions, or bell peppers to eggs or egg whites.
• At lunch, have a cup of vegetable soup or a salad with your meal.
• At dinner, include an extra serving or two of vegetables.

In between meals, try having a piece of fruit such as orange, peach, apple or pear, or vegetables like celery, cucumber, carrots, tomatoes, or bell pepper. Meal dynamics is a way of saying that it's not just what you eat and when you eat that matters; how you eat matters, too! There are few variables in how one eats.

Your sequence: Main dish, salads, then dessert? How about having dessert first to guarantee that there is still room, instead of filling it all up? It is vital to deliberate on how customs lead us and to know whether it all makes sense. If you learn to yourself you want to have dessert, why not eat it first so you'll have time to relish it instead of stuffing it in when you're full?

Pace and duration: Are the meal more like a tweet or an essay? Is it more evocative of a furious choreography or ballroom dance? How long does it take to consume the meal?

Timing: If you have an AC eating schedule on your meals, do you eat your meal at the start of the eating window? Or at the end? Or do you nibble snack portion of foods through the window? Does it change anything if you eat carbohydrates first or last?

It can also be introduced that eating too heavy and too late promotes bad dreams, and the body focuses only on digestion and not on the regenerative processes of the body such as: skin renewal, treatment of infections and injuries of the body, hormones of satiety are not produced, the same as when you consume too much alcohol before going to bed.

Fast food may be adding to surplus fat in ways that go beyond being loaded with calories and engineered to have a compelling, appetite-stimulating taste and mouthfeel. Fast food is fast in another way: not only is it available quickly, but people tend to eat it and digest it promptly with complete absorption. The suitability of snacks such as burgers, smoothies, and fries help you achieve your calorie intake worth for a day in those 10 minutes of eating them. With all of those calories flowing down to your throat, you won't be able to measure your calorie intake from the first bite of your meal. You just paid for the meal, so you eat every edge to get the maximum value. It may not be ideal, because those extra bites expand your stomach, so it will allow you to eat more food later on to have that same feeling of fullness. Stomach stretch is a viral sensation that helps you know when you've had enough; it prevents you from spraining your stomach by savoring those extra bites. You get your superior value by having those different bites later, if not necessary, getting rid of those excess calories is still better than stuffing it into your body. Be mindful of ordering meals to avoid left-overs.

To use meal dynamics as a tool, you:

1. Eat low-calorie, high-volume foods first: Soups and salads are great for this for reasons mentioned in the "Meal Composition" section. Besides soups and salads, you can snack on pickles, cucumbers, celery, carrots, grape tomatoes, and other low-calorie foods with high water content instead of concentrated calorie juice, nuts, chips, or rapidly digested foods. Remember the Super-BCPs? (Sugars, pasta, rice, bread, cereal, and potatoes).

2. Nutrition experts say that you should focus on food by consciously sniffing and tasting so that your body can record the act of eating.

Take your time! Meals are not a pit stop where every second you reduce your eating time is an advantage for the daily rush.

Enjoy the aromas and the company of other people...

And if you have to eat alone, don't get tangled up in other activities at the same time. Do not chew or swallow hastily.
Bon appetite! If you take less than half an hour to eat, don't let your stomach and brain record everything you've eaten.
The dynamic of eating is to listen to your body and feel the natural feeling of satiety.
Even if you eat fast food, you can correct your appetite by eating it slowly.

Energizing Smoothie & Milk Shake Recipes

Peach Perfection Smoothie

Preparation Time: 5 minutes
Cooking Time: 0 minutes
Servings: 2

Ingredients:

- ½ cup frozen mangos
- 1 cup frozen peaches
- ½ cup frozen strawberries
- ¼ cup apple juice
- ½ cup peach juice
- ¼ cup strawberry juice
- 1 cup ice

Directions:

1. Put all the ingredients and fill it to the max water line, then blend until smooth.

Nutrition:

509 Calories, 31g Fats, 4g Fiber

My notes:

Strawberry Raspberry Banana Smoothie

Preparation Time: 5 minutes

Cooking Time: 0 minutes

Servings: 2

Ingredients:

- ½ banana, sliced
- ½ cup frozen raspberries
- ½ cup frozen strawberries
- ½ cup apple juice
- ½ cup strawberry juice
- ½ cup soy milk
- 1 cup ice

Directions:

1. Put all the ingredients and fill it to the max water line, then blend until smooth.

Nutrition:

488 Calories, 29g Fats, 4g Protein

My notes:

Mango-A-Go-Go Smoothie

Preparation Time: 5 minutes
Cooking Time: 0 minutes
Servings: 2

Ingredients:
- 1 cup frozen mangos
- 1 cup passion fruit-mango juice
- 1 cup pineapple sherbet
- 1 cup ice

Directions:
1. Put all the ingredients and fill it to the max water line, then blend until smooth.

Nutrition:
501 Calories, 28g Fats, 4g Fiber

My notes:

Jamba Juice: Protein Berry Workout

Preparation Time: 5 minutes
Cooking Time: 0 minutes
Servings: 2

Ingredients:
- 1 cup vanilla soy milk
- 1 scoop vanilla protein powder desired brand
- 1 cup frozen strawberries
- 1 frozen banana sliced (slice before freezing)
- 1 cup ice

Directions:
1. Put all the ingredients and fill it to the max water line, then blend until smooth.

Nutrition:
418 Calories, 24g Fats, 5g Fiber

My notes:

Homemade Strawberry-mango Smoothie

Preparation Time: 5 minutes
Cooking Time: 0 minutes
Servings: 2

Ingredients:

- 1 cup sliced strawberries
- 1 cup chopped mango
- 6 ounces Greek yogurt
- 6-8 ice cubes
- ½ banana, sliced
- ½ cup frozen raspberries

Directions:

1. Place the strawberries and yogurt in a blender.
2. Place the mango, and yogurt in another blender.
3. Blend ingredients at high speed, adding ice cubes and until smooth.
4. Pour smoothies in two or more layers into glasses and garnish with banana pieces and raspberries.

Nutrition:
123 Calories, 1g Fats, 10g Protein

My notes:

Jamba Juice: Strawberry Surf Rider

Preparation Time: 5 minutes

Cooking Time: 0 minutes

Servings: 2

Ingredients:

- 1 cup lemonade
- 2 tablespoons lime juice
- ½ cup non-fat frozen yogurt
- 1 cup strawberries
- 1 cup of ice cubes

Directions:

1. Put all the ingredients and fill it to the max water line, then blend until smooth.

Nutrition:

440 Calories, 29g Fats, 4g Protein

My notes:

Panera Bread: Peach & Blueberry Smoothie

Preparation Time: 5 minutes
Cooking Time: 0 minutes
Servings: 2

Ingredients:
- ¼ cup frozen blueberries
- 1 small frozen peach, pitted and sliced (slice before freezing)
- ½ frozen banana, sliced (slice before freezing)
- ¾ cup unsweetened almond milk
- ½ cup fresh orange juice

Directions:
1. Put all the ingredients and fill it to the max water line, then blend until smooth.

Nutrition:
600 Calories, 19g Fats, 6g Fiber

My notes:

Panera's Copycat Mango Smoothie

Preparation Time: 10 minutes
Cooking Time: 0 minutes
Servings: 2

Ingredients:

- 2 cups frozen peeled mangoes, chopped
- ½ cup unsweetened pineapple juice
- ½ medium ripe banana
- 1 tablespoon honey
- ½ cup reduced-fat plain yogurt

Directions:

1. Blend all the ingredients until smooth. Pour into serving glasses and serve chilled.

Nutrition:
657 Calories, 36g Fats, 6g Protein

My notes:

Naked Juice: Green Machine Smoothie

Preparation Time: 5 minutes
Cooking Time: 0 minutes
Servings: 2

Ingredients:
- 2 green apples, peeled and cored
- ¾ cup fresh broccoli florets
- ½ cup frozen mango chunks
- 1 cup pineapple juice
- ¼ cup apple juice
- 1 cup baby spinach
- 4 kale leaves, stems removed
- 1 kiwi, peeled, sliced
- 1 small frozen banana, sliced

Directions:
1. Put all the ingredients and fill it to the max water line, then blend until smooth.

Nutrition:
391 Calories, 5g Fiber, 19g Fats

My notes:

Naked Juice: Red Machine

Preparation Time: 5 minutes
Cooking Time: 0 minutes
Servings: 2

Ingredients:
- 1 red apple, peeled, cored, and chopped
- ½ cup raspberries
- ½ frozen banana, sliced (slice before freezing)
- ¼ cup fresh pomegranate juice
- ¼ cup blood orange juice
- 4 fresh cranberries
- ¼ cup red grapes
- 3-4 ice cubes

Directions:
1. Put all the ingredients and fill it to the max water line, then blend until smooth.

Nutrition:
601 Calories, 14g Fats, 3g Fiber

My notes:

Cookies & Cream Shake

Preparation Time: 5 minutes
Cooking Time: 0 minutes
Servings: 2

Ingredients:
- 6 Oreo cookies
- 2 ½ cups French vanilla ice cream, softened
- 1/4 cup milk
- 2 teaspoons vanilla extract
- whipped cream, optional
- 2 maraschino cherries, optional

Directions:
1. Break the cookies into a blender, and add the ice cream, milk, and vanilla extract.
2. Blend until smooth.
3. Pour into two glasses and garnish each with whipped cream and a maraschino cherry.

Nutrition:
461 Calories, 22g Fats, 7g Protein

My notes:

McDonald's Copycat Shamrock Shake

Preparation Time: 10 minutes

Cooking Time: 0 minutes

Servings: 3

Ingredients:

- 3cups vanilla ice cream
- 1 cup whole milk
- 1/4 teaspoon mint extract
- 9 drops food coloring
- whipped cream
- green sanding sugar
- maraschino cherries

Directions:

1. Put the ice cream in the blender, add one by one the milk, mint extract, food coloring, and mix.
2. Pour into three glasses adding the whipped cream, powdered sugar, and a cherry.

Nutrition:

323 Calories, 17g Fats, 7g Protein

My notes:

Wendy's Copycat Chocolate Frosty

Preparation Time: 1 hour 20 minutes
Cooking Time: 0 minutes
Servings: 2

Ingredients:
- ½ cup chocolate syrup
- 2 cups whole milk
- 1 (7-ounce) can sweetened condensed milk
- ½ teaspoon vanilla extract
- ½ cup heavy cream

Directions:
1. Combine the chocolate syrup, whole milk, and condensed milk in a mixing bowl. Refrigerate for 1 hour until chilled.
2. To another mixing bowl, add the heavy cream and vanilla. Beat well until soft peaks form. Chill in the refrigerator.
3. Ready your ice cream maker and add the chocolate mixture to the ice cream making bowl. Prepare ice cream as per instructions (it will take about 15–20 minutes to churn it). Turn off the machine, take out the paddles, and add the cream mixture to the bowl. Combine well. Serve chilled, or place in the freezer until frozen to the desired consistency.

Nutrition:
509 Calories, 29g Fats, 8g Protein

My notes:

Jack in The Box's Copycat Pumpkin Pie Shake

Preparation Time: 10 minutes
Cooking Time: 0 minutes
Servings: 2

Ingredients:

- 3 tablespoons sugar
- ¾ cup whole milk
- 3 cups vanilla ice cream
- ¾ teaspoon pumpkin pie spice
- ¾ cup canned pumpkin
- 2 maraschino cherries and whipped cream to garnish

Directions:

1. Add the milk and sugar to a mixing bowl; mix well until the sugar dissolves. Add the pumpkin, pumpkin pie spice, ice cream, and milk mixture to a blender or food processor.
2. Blend until the mixture is smooth. Pour into two 16-ounce glasses. Serve topped with whipped cream and cherry.

Nutrition:

664 Calories, 34g Fats, 8g Protein

My notes:

Cherry & Vanilla Shake

Preparation Time 10-15 minutes

Cooking Time: 0 minutes

Servings: 2

Ingredients:
- 1¼ cup milk
- 3 servings vanilla ice cream
- 1 cup frozen cherries pitted, halved
- whipped cream to garnish

Directions:
1. Put the ice cream in the blender, add the milk, and blend until smooth

Nutrition:
130 Calories, 2g Fats, 3g Protein

My notes:

Soup Recipes

PF Chang's Hot and Sour Soup

Preparation Time: 5 minutes
Cooking Time: 5 minutes
Servings: 6

Ingredients:
- 6 ounces chicken breasts, cut into thin strips
- 1-quart chicken stock
- 1 cup soy sauce
- 1 teaspoon white pepper
- 1 (6 ounces) can bamboo shoots, cut into strips
- 6 ounces wood ear mushrooms
- ½ cup cornstarch
- ½ cup water
- 2 eggs, beaten
- ½ cup white vinegar
- 6 ounces silken tofu, cut into strips
- Sliced green onions for garnish

Directions:
1. Cook the chicken strips in a hot skillet until cooked through. Set aside. Add the chicken stock, soy sauce, pepper, and bamboo shoots to a stockpot and bring to a boil. Stir in the chicken and let cook for about 3–4 minutes.

2. In a small dish, make a slurry with the cornstarch and water. Add a bit at a time to the stockpot until the broth thickens to your desired consistency.

3. Stir in the beaten eggs and cook for about 45 seconds or until the eggs are done.

4. Remove from the heat and add the vinegar and tofu. Garnish with sliced green onions.

Nutrition:

228 Calories, 14g Fat, 13g Carbs, 13g Protein

My notes:

Disneyland's Monterey Clam Chowder

Preparation Time: 15 minutes
Cooking Time: 60 minutes
Servings: 2

Ingredients:
- 5 tablespoons butter
- 5 tablespoons flour
- 2 tablespoons vegetable oil
- 1½ cups potatoes (peeled, diced)
- ½ cup onion, diced
- ½ cup red pepper
- ½ cup green pepper
- ½ cup celery
- 2¼ cups clam juice
- 1½ cups heavy cream
- 1 cup clams, chopped
- 1 tablespoon fresh thyme
- ¼–½ teaspoon salt
- 1 pinch white pepper
- ⅓–½ teaspoon Tabasco sauce
- 4 individual sourdough round breads made into bowls
- Chives for garnish (optional)

Directions:
1. Make a roux by mixing melted butter and flour over medium heat for 10 minutes. Flour burns quickly, so make sure to watch the mixture closely. Set the roux aside.
2. Sauté the potatoes, onions, peppers, and celery in the oil for 10 minutes using a soup pot.
3. Whisk the rest of the ingredients, including the roux, into the soup pot, and bring the entire mixture to a boil.
4. After the mixture has boiled, reduce the heat and let it simmer for another 5 minutes.

5. Season the soup as you like with salt and pepper. To serve, ladle the soup evenly into the prepared bread bowls and sprinkle with fresh chives if desired.

Nutrition:
472.3 Calories, 36.9g Fat, 27.4g Carbs, 9.3g Protein
Sodium: 771.5 mg

My notes:

Outback's Baked Potato Soup

Preparation Time: 15 minutes
Cooking Time: 40 minutes
Servings: 2

Ingredients:

- 2 quarts water
- 8 medium-sized potatoes, cut into chunks
- 4 cans chicken broth
- 1 small onion, minced
- 1 teaspoon salt
- 1 teaspoon ground pepper
- 2 cups cold water
- 1 cup butter
- ¾ cup flour
- 1½ cup heavy cream
- 1½ cups jack cheese
- 2-3 thick-cut bacon slices, cooked and diced
- ¼ cup green onion, minced

Directions:

1. In a pot, add water and potatoes. Bring to a boil, reduce heat to medium, and cook potatoes for 10-15 minutes or until for tender. Drain and set aside.

2. In a separate pot, pour in broth and mix in onions, salt, pepper, and water. Simmer for 20 minutes.

3. Meanwhile, in another pot, whisk together butter and flour. Slowly add this to the pot of broth. Stir in heavy cream to the mixture and simmer for 20 minutes. Mix in potatoes to reheat.
4. Sprinkle jack cheese, bacon bits, and green onions on top. Serve.

Nutrition:

845 Calories, 49g Fats, 81g Carbs, 23g Protein

My notes:

Applebee's Tomato Basil Soup

Preparation Time: 15 minutes
Cooking Time: 20 minutes
Servings: 2

Ingredients:

- 3 tablespoons olive oil
- 1 small garlic clove, finely chopped
- 1 10 ¾-ounce can condense tomato
- ¼ cup bottled marinara sauce
- 5 ounces water
- 1 teaspoon fresh oregano, diced
- ½ teaspoon ground black pepper
- 1 tablespoon fresh basil, diced
- 6 Italian-style seasoned croutons
- 2 tablespoons Parmesan cheese, shredded

Directions:

1. Heat oil in a pan over medium heat. Add garlic and stir fry for 2 to 3 minutes or until garlic is soft and aromatic.
2. Pour tomato soup and marinara sauce into a pan and stir. Add water gradually. Toss in oregano and pepper. Once simmering, reduce heat to low. Cook for about 15 more minutes until all the flavors are combined. Add basil and stir.

3. Transfer to bowls. Add croutons on top and sprinkle with Parmesan cheese. Serve.

Nutrition:
350 Calories, 26g Fats, 28g Carbs, 2g Fibers

Recipes for Bread

Red Robin Burger

Preparation Time: 10 minutes
Cooking Time: 30 minutes
Servings: 4

Ingredients:

- 4 toasted buns or 4 toast
- 1 ½ pounds lean hamburger
- 4 large eggs, fried over-medium
- Fresh coarse ground black pepper & seasoning salt to taste
- 8 slices American cheese
- ketchup
- 4 slices bacon, cooked and cut in half
- Fresh lettuce
- 4 slices tomatoes
- Mayonnaise

Directions:

1. Cook the bacon until done; set aside to cool. Once done, break into half. Make 4 even-sized patties of beef and then season with pepper and salt to taste; pan-fry or grill in a small amount of bacon fat until done.
2. Place each patty with a slice of cheese, cover lightly & set aside. Fry the eggs to your liking sunny-side up, over medium heat. Toast the buns. Once the eggs are done, set them aside. Assemble your burger in the following order:

3. Bottom bun followed by a slice of cheese, fried egg, a small amount of ketchup, 2 pieces of bacon, tomato, fresh lettuce & top the bun, spread with mayo.
4. Serve with French fries or hash browns and enjoy.

Nutrition:
904 Calories, 62.4g Fats, 40.1g Protein

My notes:

Sautéed Mushroom Burger

Preparation Time: 10 minutes
Cooking Time: 20 minutes
Servings: 4

Ingredients:
- 1 lb. ground hamburger
- Garlic salt to taste
- Onion powder to taste
- Seasoned salt to taste
- 2 c. sliced mushrooms
- 1 tbsp. butter
- ½ onion caramelized
- 4 slices Swiss cheese
- Lettuce

Directions:
1. Preheat your grill over medium-high heat. Evenly divide the hamburger into eight balls. Flatten & season both sides with pepper & salt to taste. Grill until you get your desired doneness. Once done, remove them from the heat. Caramelize the onions & sauté the mushrooms with butter until tender; set aside. Once the burger is done, top with onions, lettuce, mushrooms, & cheese.

Nutrition:
891 Calories, 58.9g Fats, 37.9g Protein

My notes:

Whisky River Burger

Preparation Time: 20 minutes
Cooking Time: 20 minutes
Servings: 6

Ingredients:

- 2 pounds 80/20 ground beef
- 6 slices of cheddar cheese
- Oil, for brushing the burgers
- 12 tablespoon mayonnaise
- Onion rings, thin & crispy
- 6 seeded hamburger buns
- Bourbon whiskey BBQ sauce
- 2 cups fresh lettuce, chopped
- 12 slices tomato

Directions:

1. Preheat the charcoal grill over high heat until it glows bright orange & ashes over.
2. In the meantime, make 6 even-sized patties from the ground beef. Lightly brush the burgers with oil.
3. Grill the burgers for a couple of minutes until turn browned & slightly charred on the first side. Flip & continue cooking until you get your desired level of doneness. Drizzle the Bourbon Whiskey BBQ Sauce over the burgers & place one slice of cheese on each burger. Cook until the cheese just starts to melt, for a minute more. Remove from the heat; set aside, and assemble the burgers.
4. Layer the cut side of both sides of the sandwich with about 1 tablespoon of mayonnaise on each half. Place the onion rings add the burger with the cheese, sauce, lettuce, and tomatoes.

Nutrition:
893 Calories, 57.8g Fats, 40.4g Protein

Tuscan Butter Burger

Preparation Time: 15 minutes
Cooking Time: 30 minutes
Servings: 4

Ingredients:
For the Chicken Burgers:
- 1 cup panko
- 1 ½ pounds ground chicken
- 4 green onions, minced
- 2 tablespoon extra-virgin olive oil
- 1 teaspoon Himalayan pink salt, black pepper, garlic blend

For the Tuscan Butter Sauce:
- ¼ cup Parmesan, finely grated
- 2 tablespoon butter
- ½ cup heavy cream
- 1 tablespoon tomato paste
- ¼ teaspoon Himalayan pink salt, black pepper, garlic blend

For Assembly:
- 4 seeded hamburger buns, split & lightly toasted
- 1 cup large basil leaves, fresh
- 1 jar oil-packed sun-dried tomatoes (7-ounces), drained

Directions:
For Chicken Burgers:
1. Combine the chicken together with panko, green onions & 1 teaspoon Himalayan pink salt, garlic blend, black pepper in a medium bowl.
2. Cook oil over medium-high heat in a large skillet. Form 4 even-sized patties from the chicken mixture using slightly dampened hands, placing the patties carefully into the hot skillet. Cook for 8 to 10 minutes, until turn golden, flipping once during the Cooking Time. Remove the patties to a large plate; drain any excess oil.

For Tuscan butter Sauce:

3. Place the skillet over medium-low heat & add butter & tomato paste. Cook for a minute, whisking frequently. Whisk in the Parmesan, heavy cream & ¼ teaspoon Himalayan pink salt, black pepper, garlic blend. Bring the mixture to a simmer. Once done, decrease the heat to low & let simmer until parmesan is melted & the sauce is reduced slightly, for a couple of more minutes. Remove from the heat.

4. Place the burger patties on the bottom buns. Spoon the Tuscan butter sauce on top of patties and then top with sun-dried tomatoes and basil. Close the sandwich with the top bun.

Nutrition:

897 Calories, 60g Fats, 40g Protein

My notes:

Four Cheese Melt

Preparation Time: 10 minutes
Cooking Time: 30 minutes
Servings: 4

Ingredients:

- 1 cup Asiago, shredded
- 2 tablespoons extra-virgin olive oil, 2 turns of the pan
- 1 garlic clove, cracked away from the skin
- 8 slices of crusty Italian semolina bread
- 1 cup mozzarella, shredded
- ½ cup Romano or Parmesan, grated
- 1 cup provolone, shredded
- 3 tablespoons butter

Directions:

1. Over medium-low heat in a small skillet; heat the oil with butter. Once the butter is completely melted, add the garlic & gently cook for 2 to 3 minutes. Remove the garlic butter mixture from heat.
2. Now, over medium-high heat in a large nonstick skillet. Brush 1 side of 4 slices of bread with garlic oil using a pastry brush & place the buttered side down into the hot skillet. Top each slice with equal amounts of the 4 cheeses; evenly distributing them over the 4 slices. Top each sandwich with a slice more of bread brushed with garlic butter, buttered side up.

Flip the grill cheese sandwiches a couple of times until cheeses are melted & gooey and the bread is toasty & golden. Cut grilled 4 cheese sandwiches from corner to corner; serve and enjoy.

Nutrition:
904 Calories, 61g Fats, 40.9g Protein

My notes:

The Boss Burger

Preparation Time: 15 minutes
Cooking Time: 25 minutes
Servings: 3

Ingredients:

- 1-pound ground beef
- 3 cheese slices
- Worcestershire sauce
- 3 fried eggs
- canned green chilis or
  Verde green sauce (any of your favorite)
- 6 bacon slices, cooked until crisp
- Pico de Gallo
- 3 burger buns
- Pepper & salt to taste

Directions:

1. Heat your grill over high heat. Season the ground beef with dashes of Worcestershire sauce, pepper & salt. Make 3 patties from the mixture & cook until you get your desired level of doneness. During the last minute of your Cooking Time, top each burger with a cheese slice. Place on a bun topped with an egg, bacon, a big scoop of Pico de Gallo & a scoop of Verde sauce.
2. Serve immediately & enjoy.

Nutrition:

889 Calories, 60g Fats, 40g Protein

Alex's Santa Fe Burger

Preparation Time: 15 minutes
Cooking Time: 15 minutes
Servings: 4

Ingredients:
For Burgers:

- 12 yellow or blue corn tortilla chips
- 1 poblano chili, large
- 4 hamburger buns, split; toasted
- 1 ½ pounds 80% lean ground chuck or 90% lean ground turkey
- 2 ½ tablespoons canola oil
- Freshly ground black pepper & kosher salt to taste

For Queso Sauce:

- 1 tablespoon all-purpose flour
- 2 cups Monterey Jack cheese, coarsely grated (approximately 8 ounces)
- 1 tablespoon unsalted butter
- 1 ½ cups whole milk
- Freshly ground black pepper & kosher salt to taste

Directions:

1. Preheat oven to 375 F. Put the chili on a rimmed baking sheet; rub with a tablespoon of the oil & then season with pepper and salt to taste. Roast in the preheated oven for 12 to 15 minutes until the skin of the chili is blackened. Remove & place the chili in a large bowl; cover using a plastic wrap & let steam for 12 to 15 more minutes. Peel, stem & seed the chili, then chop it coarsely.

For Queso Sauce:

2. Heat the butter over medium heat in a small saucepan until completely melted. Whisk in the flour & cook for a minute. Add the milk; stir well and increase the heat to high; cook for 3 to 5 minutes, until thickened slightly, whisking constantly. Remove from

the heat & whisk in the cheese until melted, then season with pepper and salt. Try to keep it warm.

3. Evenly divide the meat into 4 portions. Loosely form each portion into a ¾" thick burger & make a deep depression in the middle with your thumb. Season both sides of each burger with pepper and salt. Cook the burgers in the leftover oil.

4. Place the burgers on the bun bottoms & top each with chips, a few tablespoons of queso sauce & some poblano. Cover with the bun tops; serve immediately & enjoy.

For Toasted Burger Buns:

5. To toast a bun on a grill, griddle or grill pan; split the bun open and place it on the grill, cut side down; grill for a couple of seconds, until turn golden brown lightly.

Nutrition:

891 Calories, 62g Fats, 41g Protein

My notes:

The Southern Charm Burger

Preparation Time: 15 minutes
Cooking Time: 30 minutes
Servings: 4

Ingredients:

- 2 pounds ground bison or beef
- 1 tablespoon Texas Pete or Tabasco
- 4 garlic cloves, minced
- 1 small onion, minced
- BBQ Sauce with Honey and Molasses for basting
- 8 ounces container pimento cheese spread
- 1 large green tomato, cut into 8 slices
- ¼ cup corn meal, seasoned with salt and pepper
- 1 large egg, beaten
- Pickled okra for condiments
- 8 Hearty Buns
- Nonstick cooking spray

Directions:

1. Preheat the oven to 350 degrees. Mix the egg with a small amount of water in a shallow bowl & then season with pepper and salt to taste. Place the corn meal out onto a medium-sized plate.
2. Before cooking, soak the tomato slices into the egg and then press into the corn meal; ensure that the outside is nicely coated. Place the slices onto the baking sheet lightly coated with the cooking spray. Spray tops of tomatoes with the cooking spray. Bake for 12 to 15 minutes, until golden brown, turning once during the baking process.
3. Combine the ground beef together with onions, tabasco, and garlic in a large-sized mixing bowl. Season the meat well; combine thoroughly. Make 8 even-sized patties from the mixture. Baste with the BBQ Sauce & grill until you get your desired doneness.

4. Just about a minute before you remove the patties from the grill, place a portion of pimento cheese spread on top of burgers using a cookie scoop. For even melting, press the cheese down using a large spatula. Place one "fried" green tomato over each bun, top with burger, and garnish with your favorite condiments.

Nutrition:
893 Calories, 58g Fats, 40g Protein

My notes:

Chili's Avocado Beef Burger

Preparation Time: 20 minutes
Cooking Time: 20 minutes
Servings: 4

Ingredients:

- 1-pound ground beef
- 8 sliced crispy cooked bacon
- 1 teaspoon Worcestershire sauce
- Tomato slices
- ¼ teaspoon dried thyme
- Onion Slices
- 1 teaspoon Tabasco sauce
- 4 slices of American cheese
- Mayonnaise
- 2 avocados
- Fresh Lettuce
- 4 sesame burger buns
- Pepper & salt to taste

Directions:

1. Season the ground beef with Tabasco, Worcestershire sauce, thyme, pepper, and salt. Lightly toss the ingredients using a fork until combined well. Make 4 palm-sized beef patties from the mixture.
2. Prepare your grill pan over moderate heat. When done, place the beef patty over the pan & grill until you get your desired level of

doneness, for 4 to 5 minutes per side. In the meantime, mash the avocado & season with pepper and salt. Add a small amount of spice, if desired.

3. When done, layer the bottom half of the bun with the mayonnaise, onion, lettuce and tomato. Add the hot beef patty on top & then add on the cheese. Layer it with avocado & finally, a few pieces of crispy bacon. Top it off with the top of the bun; serve immediately & enjoy.

Nutrition:

907 Calories, 61g Fats, 40g Protein

My notes:

Tuna Salad Wraps

Preparation Time: 5 minutes
Cooking Time: 15 minutes
Servings: 4

Ingredients:

- 1 (11-ounce) pouch tuna in water
- 1 cup parsley leaves, chopped
- ¼ cup mint leaves, chopped
- ¼ cup minced shallot
- 1½ teaspoons sumac
- 1 teaspoon Dijon mustard
- 1 tablespoon olive oil
- 1 tablespoon freshly squeezed lemon juice
- ¼ cup unsalted sunflower seeds
- 16 large or medium romaine or bibb lettuce leaves
- 1 red bell pepper, cut into thin sticks (3 to 4 inches long)
- 3 Persian cucumbers, cut into thin sticks (3 to 4 inches long)

Directions:

1. In a large bowl, mix together the tuna, parsley, mint, shallot, sumac, mustard, oil, lemon juice, and sunflower seeds.
2. Place ¾ cup of tuna salad in each of 4 containers.

3. Place 4 lettuce leaves, one-quarter of the peppers, and one-quarter of the cucumbers in each of 4 separate containers so that they don't get soggy from the tuna salad.

Nutrition:

223 Calories, 9g Fats, 24g Protein

My notes:

Ranchero Chicken Tacos

My notes:

Preparation Time: 15 minutes
Cooking Time: 15 minutes
Servings: 8

Ingredients:
- Cheddar cheese, shredded
- Flour tortillas
- Chicken breast, sliced

For Ranchero Sauce:
- 2 garlic cloves, chopped
- 1 Serrano or jalapeno chili, seeded & diced
- ¼ cup of chopped onion
- 3 cups tomatoes, diced
- ½ teaspoon ground chili
- 1 tablespoon oregano
- 2 tablespoons cooking oil

Directions:
For Ranchero Sauce:
1. Over moderate heat in a large saucepan; heat the oil until hot & then sauté the onions, garlic, and Serrano for a couple of minutes.
2. Decrease the heat & add in the tomatoes; stir well & cook until the tomatoes have wilted for 5 to 6 minutes. Add the seasonings & let simmer for 5 minutes more.

For Quesadilla:
3. Sauté or grill the chicken. Mix the chicken with the prepared sauce. Butter the outside of your tortilla. Add the chicken-ranchero sauce filling and cheese. Fold the tortilla & cook in a hot skillet. Serve hot & enjoy.

Nutrition:
869 Calories, 58g Fats, 38g Protein

Mushroom Jack Chicken Fajitas

Preparation Time: 10 minutes
Cooking Time: 45 minutes
Servings: 4

Ingredients:
For Chipotle Garlic Butter:
- 8 garlic cloves, finely minced
- ¼ cup canned chipotle peppers
- 1 teaspoon each of ground black pepper & salt
- ⅓ cup unsalted butter, softened

For Caramelized Onions:
- 1 ½ tablespoons white sugar
- 6 medium yellow or white onions; sliced into ¼ to ½" thick slices; separating them into rings
- 1 ½ tablespoons balsamic vinegar
- ¼ cup vegetable stock
- 1 ½ tablespoons butter, unsalted
- ½ teaspoon salt
- 1 ½ tablespoons vegetable oil

For Fajitas:
- 2 pounds chicken breast, boneless and skinless
- 1 tablespoon chipotle powder
- 2 tablespoons Cajun seasoning
- 1 teaspoon ground black pepper
- 2 cups green peppers

- ⅓ cup fresh cilantro, minced
- 2 tablespoons vegetable oil
- 1 cup Monterey Jack cheese, shredded
- 2 cups cremini mushrooms, sliced
- ½ cup green onion, minced
- Ground black pepper & salt to taste
- 2 tablespoons lime juice, freshly squeezed
- 1 ½ teaspoons salt

To Serve:
- ½ cup sour cream
- 12 corn or flour tortillas
- ¼ cup canned jalapeños, sliced
- 1 cup Monterey Jack cheese, shredded
- ¼ cup guacamole

Directions:

Caramelize the Onions:

1. Over moderate heat in a shallow pan; heat the butter until melted. Scatter the sliced onions on top of the melted butter and then drizzle with the oil; slowly cook for 8 to 10 minutes, until turn translucent.

2. Decrease the heat to medium-low; give the onions a good stir and add the vinegar and sugar; toss & stir until mixed well.

3. After 10 minutes of cooking, pour in the broth. To prevent the onions from burning, don't forget to scrape up any caramelized bits from the bottom of your pan & stir every now and then.

4. Once the onions are browned well & very soft, after 10 to 15 minutes more of cooking, remove them from the heat.

Preparing the Butter:

5. Now, over medium heat in a small saucepan, heat 2 tablespoons of the butter until melted and then add the minced garlic; cook for 8 to 10 minutes, until the garlic turns fragrant and begins to brown.

6. Remove the butter from heat and place in the fridge until chilled, for 15 minutes. In a small bowl, combine the garlic butter together with softened butter, chipotle & salt.

7. Mash all the ingredients together using a large fork. Season the mixture with more salt & ground black pepper, if required. Using a plastic wrap, cover the seasoned butter & store it in the fridge until ready to use.

For the Fajitas:

8. Slice the chicken breast into ½" strips, rubbing them with the chipotle powder, Cajun seasoning, lime juice, pepper, and salt. Let rest while you heat the pan.

9. Now, over high heat in a cast iron pan; heat half of the oil until it starts to shimmer, add half of the chicken strips; cook until cooked through & well-browned. Transfer the cooked chicken to a plate & cook the leftover chicken strips.

10. Add the sliced mushrooms to the hot pan; ensure that you don't add more of oil or rinse the mushrooms. Bring the heat to medium-high & cook until the mushrooms turn brown & begin to crisp, undisturbed. Sprinkle them with a very small quantity of salt.

11. Carefully flip the mushrooms & continue to cook for 5 to 7 more minutes, until both sides turn browned & they are completely cooked. Transfer them to the plate with the cooked chicken.

12. Add the leftover oil to the hot pan. When it starts to shimmer and starts to smoke, add in the green peppers & lightly sprinkle them with a very small amount of salt, stirring occasionally.

13. When the peppers begin to soften, push them so that they sit around the edge of the pan; decrease the heat to low.

14. Add the caramelized onions to the middle of your pan, pushing them so that the peppers and onions cover any exposed portions of the pan.

15. Place the cooked chicken strips over the onions. Dot the onions, peppers, and chicken with the chipotle butter sauce.

16. Sprinkle the chicken with the shredded cheese. Layer the cooked mushrooms on top of the cheese & dot the mushrooms with ½ to 1 tablespoon more of butter.

17. Cover the pan with a lid & let it sit for 5 minutes on low heat. Once the chicken is warmed through & the cheese is completely melted, scatter the cilantro and green onions on top.

18. Serve the fajitas immediately in the cast iron pan. Warm the tortillas & serve the salsa, jalapeños, sour cream, guacamole, and extra cheese on the side.

Nutrition:

894 Calories, 60.9g Fats, 40.9g Protein

My notes:

Greek Chicken Wraps

Preparation Time: 5 minutes
Cooking Time: 15 minutes
Servings: 2

Ingredients:
For the Filling:

- 2 chicken breasts 14 oz, chopped into 1-inch pieces
- 2 small zucchinis, cut into 1-inch pieces
- 2 bell peppers, cut into 1-inch pieces
- 1 red onion, cut into 1-inch pieces
- 2 tbsp olive oil
- 2 tsp oregano
- 2 tsp basil
- 1/2 tsp garlic powder
- 1/2 tsp onion powder
- 1/2 tsp salt
- 2 lemons, sliced

To Serve:

- 1/4 cup feta cheese crumbled
- 4 large flour tortillas or wraps

Directions:

1. preheat oven to 425 degrees F.
2. In a bowl, mix chicken, zucchini, olive oil, oregano, basil, garlic, bell pepper, onion powder, salt
3. Place a lemon slice on the baking sheet(s), spread chicken and vegetables on top (use 2 baking sheets if necessary)
4. Bake chicken and vegetables for 15 minutes
5. Allow to cool completely

6. Distribute the chicken, peppers, zucchini, and onions among the containers and remove the lemon slices
7. sprinkle with feta cheese
8. enjoy hot or cold

Nutrition:

356 Calories, 14g Fats, 29g Protein

My notes:

Chicken Quesadillas

Preparation Time: 10 minutes
Cooking Time: 15 minutes
Servings: 4

Ingredients:

- 1 1/2 tablespoon oil
- 1 1/2 tablespoons all-purpose flour
- 3/4 cup chicken stock
- 1-2 tablespoons hot sauce
- 1/4 tsp each cumin and chili powder
- salt and pepper
- 2 cups cooked, shredded chicken
- 3 cup shredded cheddar cheese
- 4 flour tortillas

Directions:

1. preheat the oven to 400 degrees and grease a rimmed baking sheet.
2. Shred the cheese and set it aside.
3. Heat oil in a skillet over medium heat. Add flour and cook, stirring constantly. Slowly add broth and cook for 1-2 minutes until thickened, continuing to mix well.
4. Remove from heat and add spices, sauce, salt, pepper, chicken, and cheese, stirring thoroughly.

5. Divide the mixture evenly over each tortilla. Fold tortillas in half and place them on a baking sheet. Bake for about 8-10 minutes until golden brown and melted.

Nutrition:

498 Calories, 33g Fats, 32g Protein

My notes:

Sweet and Savory Snack Recipes

Low Fat Veggie Quesadilla

Preparation Time: 10 minutes
Cooking Time: 5 minutes
Servings: 2

Ingredients:

- ½ tablespoon canola oil
- ½ cup mushrooms, chopped
- ½ cup carrot, grated
- 1/3 cup broccoli, sliced
- 2 tablespoons onion, finely chopped
- 1 tablespoon red bell pepper, finely chopped
- 1 teaspoon soy sauce
- 1 dash cayenne pepper
- 1 dash black pepper
- 1 dash salt
- 2 flour tortillas
- ¼ cup cheddar cheese, grated
- ¼ cup mozzarella cheese, grated
- ¼ cup sour cream
- ¼ cup salsa, medium or mild to taste
- ¼ cup shredded lettuce

Directions:

1. Heat oil in a large skillet. Add mushrooms, carrots, broccoli, onion, and bell pepper. Stir-fry over medium-high heat for about 5 minutes. Pour in soy sauce, then season with cayenne, salt, and pepper. Transfer vegetables onto a plate. Set aside.
2. In the same skillet, heat first tortilla. Top with cheddar and mozzarella cheeses, followed by the cooked vegetables. Cover with the second tortilla.

Cook for about 1 minute on each side or until cheeses are runny. Cut into slices. Serve hot with sour cream, salsa, and shredded lettuce on the side.

Nutrition:
186 Calories, 12g Fats, 18g Carbs, 25g Protein

My notes:

Garlic Mashed Potatoes

My notes:

Preparation Time: 20 minutes
Cooking Time: 1 hour
Servings: 4

Ingredients:

- 1 medium-sized bulb garlic, fresh
- 2 pounds red-skinned potatoes
- ½ cup milk
- ½ cup heavy cream
- ¼ cup butter
- Salt and pepper to taste

Directions:

1. Preheat the oven to 400°F. Wrap whole garlic bulb with aluminum foil and bake it for 45 minutes, until the garlic softens. Remove it from the oven and let it cool in its wrapping.
2. Once cool, unwrap the garlic, peel off the outer layer, and squeeze the cooked pulp out. Set it aside. In the meantime, cut the potatoes and wash them, don't remove the skin and put them in a saucepan. Add water just to cover the potatoes. Boil until it cooks thoroughly for about 20 minutes.
3. Drain the water and add the other ingredients. Use the hands to mash. Lumps can be left, depending on your preference. Serve.

Nutrition:

254 Calories, 6g Fats, 24g Carbs, 31g Protein

Vegetable Medley

Preparation Time: 15 minutes
Cooking Time: 10 minutes
Servings: 4

Ingredients

- ½ pound cold, fresh zucchini sliced in half-moons
- ½ pound cold, fresh yellow squash, sliced in half-moons
- ¼ pound cold red pepper, julienned in strips ¼-inch thick
- ¼ pound cold carrots, cut into ¼-inch strips a few inches long
- ¼ pound cold red onions, thinly sliced
- 1 cold, small corn cob, cut crosswise in 1" segments
- 3 tablespoons cold butter or margarine
- 1 teaspoon salt
- 1 teaspoon sugar
- ½ teaspoon granulated garlic
- 1 teaspoon Worcestershire sauce
- 1 teaspoon soy sauce
- 2 teaspoons fresh or dried parsley

Directions:

1. Wash, peel, and cut your vegetables as appropriate. In a saucepan, heat the butter over medium-high heat. Once it is hot, add salt, sugar, and garlic. Add the carrots, squash, and zucchini, and when they start to soften, add the rest of the vegetables and cook for a couple of minutes.

2. Add the Worcestershire sauce, soy sauce, and parsley. Stir to combine and coat the vegetables. When all the vegetables are cooked to your preference, serve.

Nutrition:
276 Calories, 21g Fats, 22g Carbs, 30g Protein

My notes:

Big Ol' Brownie

Preparation Time: 10 minutes
Cooking Time: 1 hour 10 minutes
Servings: 4

Ingredients

- 1 can of brownie mix
- Ice cream, vanilla, to serve
- Hot Caramel sauce, to serve

Directions:

Set the oven's temperature to exactly 350° F; cut the foil strips to line the giant muffin tin cups;

Lay the strips in crisscross-layer form for use as a handle for lifting when the brownies are made. Spray the foil in the kitchen spray pan; Prepare the brownie batter as indicated. Divide the batter between the muffin pans. The muffin cups can be about ¾ full;

Set the muffin pan on a heating sheet with the edges and start baking in the preheated oven for 40 to 50 minutes approximately; Remove the muffin pan from your oven and let it cool in the mold for 5 minutes approximately, then take to a rack to cool for another 10 minutes;

To loosen the sides of each brownie, you can use an icing spatula or a knife and then use the handles to lift the muffin pan. Serve a hot brownie on a plate with hot caramel sauce and a scoop of vanilla ice cream.

Nutrition:

206 Calories, 24g Fats, 24g Carbs, 29g Protein

Lasagna with Feta and Black Olives

Preparation Time: 10 minutes
Cooking Time: 15 minutes
Servings: 4

Ingredients:
- 8 lasagna sheets
- 600 gr of diced tomatoes
- Dried basil and oregano
- Salt and black pepper
- 1 sugar
- +/- 300 ml of béchamel
- 1 jar of pitted kalamata black olives
- +/- 150 gr of block feta
- A little grated cheese to brown
- A mixture of dried Greek herbs and Olive oil

Directions:
1. Heat a touch olive oil in a saucepan or frying pan. Add the diced tomatoes, sugar, dried basil and oregano, salt and pepper (dose in step with your taste). Let simmer for at least 1/2 hour. Prepare your béchamel as you commonly do. Drain the olives and dice the feta.
2. Spread a little tomato and béchamel sauce within the bottom of a gratin dish, location 2 sheets of lasagna, tomato sauce, béchamel, black olives, and diced feta. Continue identically till all the ingredients are used up. Finish with béchamel, sprinkle with grated cheese, and sprinkle with Greek herbs.
3. Finally, bake at 180 ° C for 30 to 40 minutes and serve immediately.

Nutrition:
270 Calories, 16g Fats, 11g Protein

Easy Copycat Monterey's Little Mexico Queso

Preparation Time: 15 minutes
Cooking Time: 10 minutes
Servings: 6

Ingredients:
- 1/2 cup of chopped yellow onion
- 1/2 cup of finely chopped celery
- 2 large green peppers such as Anaheim or Hatch, finely diced
- 2 tablespoons of butter
- 1 pound of American cheese
- 1/3 cup milk

Directions:
1. The real mystery of flavored cheese is to fry vegetables till they're almost wholly cooked when you begin adding a little crunch in your American cheese.
2. Place the chopped onion, thinly sliced celery, and diced pepper in a casserole over medium warmness, upload tablespoons of oil, and cook until the onion is transparent. Put in a medium bowl, American cheese, sautéed onions, and milk. Heat until low or medium warmness melts the cheese.

Nutrition
226 Calories, 4g Carbohydrates,
9g Protein, 18g Fats

My notes:

Fried Keto Cheese with Mushrooms

Preparation Time: 10 minutes
Cooking Time: 20 minutes
Servings: 4

Ingredients:

- 300 g mushrooms
- 300 g halloumi cheese
- 75 g butter 10 green olives
- salt and ground black pepper
- 125 ml mayonnaise (optional)

Directions:

1. Rinse and trim the mushrooms and chop or slice them. Heat the right quantity of butter in a pan in which they match and halloumi cheese and mushrooms.
2. Fry the mushrooms over medium heat for 3-5 minutes till golden brown. If vital, add extra butter and fry the halloumi cheese for a few minutes on every side. Stir the mushrooms occasionally.
3. Lower the warmness towards the end. Serve with olives.

Nutrition:

169 Calories, 17g Fats, 10g Protein

My notes:

Mushroom Recipe Stuffed with Cheese, Spinach, and Bacon

Preparation Time: 10 minutes
Cooking Time: 15 minutes
Servings: 4

Ingredients:

- 18 large mushrooms
- 4 strips of bacon cut into small cubes
- 2 butter spoons
- 2 tablespoons chopped onion
- ¾ cup grated fontina cheese
- 150 g spinach leaves chopped into large pieces
- Kosher Salt and freshly ground black pepper

Directions:

1. Preheat the oven to 200 ° C. Cover a baking sheet with parchment paper. Wash the mushrooms. Remove the stems and locate the lids with the rounded sides down at the baking sheet. Chop the stems and reserve.
2. In a skillet over medium warmness, fry the bacon reduce into small cubes until crispy, drains. Leave approximately a tablespoon of bacon inside the pan. Add tablespoons of butter to the pan and add the chopped mushroom stems and chopped onion. Cook until the onion is translucent.

3. Add the spinach to the pan and cook until 3 minutes. Drain and transfer the aggregate to a bowl to cool. Add the bacon and half of a cup of cheese to the slightly cooled spinach aggregate. Stir to combine the components.
4. Try and upload Salt and freshly ground black pepper. Fill the mushrooms and cover each one with a touch extra fontina cheese. Bake for 15 minutes or until cheese melts and browns slightly.

Nutrition:

164 Calories, 18g Fats, 12g Protein

My notes:

Dessert and Pastry Recipes

Campfire S'mores

Preparation Time: 15 minutes
Cooking Time: 40 minutes
Servings: 9

Ingredients:
Graham Cracker Crust:
- 2 cups graham cracker crumbs
- ¼ cup sugar
- ½ cup butter
- ½ teaspoon cinnamon
- 1 small package brownie mix (enough for an 8×8-inch pan)

Brownie Mix:
- ½ cup flour
- ⅓ cup cocoa
- ¼ teaspoon baking powder
- ¼ teaspoon salt
- ½ cup butter
- 1 cup sugar
- 1 teaspoon vanilla
- 2 large eggs

S'mores Topping:
- 9 large marshmallows
- 5 Hershey candy bars
- 4½ cups vanilla ice cream
- ½ cup chocolate sauce

Directions:
1. Preheat the oven to 350°F.
2. Mix together the graham cracker crumbs, sugar, cinnamon, and melted butter in a medium bowl. Stir until the crumbs and sugar have combined with the butter.
3. Line an 8×8-inch baking dish with parchment paper. Make sure to use enough so that you'll be able to lift the baked brownies out of

the dish easily. Press the graham cracker mixture into the bottom of the lined pan.

4. Place the pan in the oven to prebake the crust a bit while you are making the brownie mixture.

5. Melt the butter over medium heat in a large saucepan, then stir in the sugar and vanilla. Whisk in the eggs one at a time. Then whisk in the dry ingredients, followed by the nuts. Mix until smooth. Take the crust out of the oven, pour the mixture into it, and bake for 23–25 minutes. When brownies are done, remove from oven and let cool in the pan.

6. After the brownies have cooled completely, lift them out of the pan using the edges of the parchment paper. Be careful not to crack or break the brownies. Cut into individual slices.

7. When you are ready to serve, place a marshmallow on top of each brownie and broil in the oven until the marshmallow starts to brown. You can also microwave for a couple of seconds, but you won't get the browning that you would in the broiler.

8. Remove from the oven and top each brownie with half of a Hershey bar. Serve with ice cream and a drizzle of chocolate sauce.

Nutrition:
41g Carbs, 12g Fats, 4g Protein

My notes:

Banana Pudding

Preparation Time: 15 minutes + 1 hour 30 minutes chilling time
Cooking Time: 0 minutes
Servings: 8–10

Ingredients:

- 6 cups milk
- 5 eggs, beaten
- ¼ teaspoon vanilla extract
- 1⅛ cups flour
- 1½ cups sugar
- ¾ pound vanilla wafers
- 3 bananas, peeled
- 8 ounces whipped cream

Directions:

1. In a large saucepan, heat the milk to about 170°F.
2. Mix the eggs, vanilla, flour, and sugar together in a large bowl. Very slowly add the egg mixture to the warmed milk and cook until the mixture thickens to a custard consistency.
3. Layer the vanilla wafers to cover the bottom of a baking pan or glass baking dish. You can also use individual portion dessert dish or glasses.
4. Layer banana slices over the top of the vanilla wafers. Be as liberal with the bananas as you want.
5. Layer the custard mixture on top of the wafers and bananas. Move the pan to the refrigerator and cool for 1½ hours. When ready to serve, spread Cool Whip (or real whipped cream, if you prefer) over the top. Garnish with banana slices and wafers if desired.

Nutrition:
45g Carbs, 14g Fats, 3g Protein

Starbuck's Copycat Cranberry Chocolate Bliss Bars

Preparation Time: 10 minutes
Cooking Time: 55 minutes
Servings: 3 dozen

Ingredients:

- 3/4 cup of cubed butter unsalted
- 1 1/2 cups of brown sugar
- 2 eggs, large
- 3/4 tsp. of vanilla extract, pure
- 1 1/2 tsp. of baking powder
- 2 1/4 cups of flour, all-purpose
- 1/4 tsp. of salt, kosher
- 1/8 tsp. of cinnamon, ground
- 1/2 cup of cranberries, dried
- 6 oz. of chopped baking chocolate, white
- Frosting, 1 container prepared

Directions:

1. Preheat the oven to 350F. In a large-sized microwave-safe bowl, melt butter. Add and stir in brown sugar. Cool a bit.
2. Beat in vanilla and eggs. In a separate bowl, whisk flour, kosher salt, cinnamon, and baking powder together. Stir in the chocolate and cranberries, making a thick batter. Spread into buttered 13" x 9" pan. Bake till golden brown, 18 to 20 minutes or so. Completely cool on wire rack. Slice and serve.

Nutrition:

42g Carbs, 13g Fats, 3.4g Protein

Chili's New York Style Cheesecake

Preparation Time: 35 minutes

Cooking Time 1 hour 25 minutes

Servings: 12

Ingredients:

- 15 graham crackers (each 3 by 5"), broken into pieces
- 2 ½ pounds cream cheese (five 8-ounce bars), room temperature
- 1 teaspoon packed lemon zest, finely grated plus 1 tablespoon fresh juice
- ⅓ cup dark-brown sugar, packed
- 1 ⅓ cups granulated sugar
- 1 cup sour cream, at room temperature
- 5 large eggs, at room temperature
- 1 ¼ teaspoons coarse salt
- 6 tablespoons softened butter, unsalted, melted, plus more for pan
- 1 teaspoon pure vanilla extract

Directions:

1. Preheat oven to 350 F. Finely grind the crackers in a food processor. Add in the brown sugar, melted butter, zest & ½ teaspoon of salt; continue to pulse until you get wet sand-like texture. Evenly press into the bottom & halfway up sides of a buttered 9" spring form pan. Bake in the preheated oven for 12 to 15 minutes until set. Let cool.

2. Decrease your oven temperature to 325 F. Beat the cream cheese until smooth, on medium speed. Slowly beat in the granulated sugar for 2 to 3 minutes until light & fluffy. Beat in the lemon juice & leftover salt. Slowly beat in the eggs and then the vanilla and sour cream until completely smooth.

3. Place the pan in the middle of a double layer of foil. Lift the edges of foil up, tightly wrapping it around the sides of your pan & fold it in under itself until flush with the top of the pan.

4. Pour the filling into pan & smooth the top using a small offset spatula.

5. Place the springform pan in a roasting pan; transfer to the oven. Pour enough boiling water into the roasting pan to come halfway up sides of the springform pan. Bake in the preheated oven 1 hour 45 minutes to 2 hours until the cake is puffed & turn slightly wobbly in the center and golden brown on top.

6. Remove the springform pan from roasting pan; let cool for 20 minutes on a wire rack. Remove the foil and run a paring knife around the sides of the pan to loosen. Let completely cool. Drape the pan with a plastic wrap; refrigerate for overnight until cold. Remove the cake from pan; serve & enjoy.

Nutrition:

44g Carbs, 12g Fats, 3.9g Protein

My notes:

Chocolate Pecan Pie

Preparation Time: 15 minutes
Cooking Time: 50 minutes
Servings: 12

Ingredients:

- 4 eggs
- 6 ounces coarsely chopped chocolate
- 1/2 cup melted unsalted butter
- 2 tablespoons unsweetened cocoa powder
- 3/4 cup maple syrup
- 3/4 cup light brown sugar packaged
- 2 tablespoons all-purpose flour
- 1 tablespoon pure vanilla extract
- 2 cups pecans
- 1/2 cup unsalted butter melted
- 2 tablespoons unsweetened cocoa powder
- 3/4 cup maple syrup,
- 3/4 cup light brown sugar packed
- 2 tablespoons all-purpose flour
- 1 tablespoon pure vanilla extract
- 2 cup pecans
- 3/4 teaspoon salt
- 1 unbaked pie shell

Directions:

1. Preheat the oven to 350°F with the rack in the lowest position.
2. prick the base a few times with a fork to avoid air bubbles before pouring in the filling.
3. toast the pecans on a baking sheet for 10 minutes.
4. Reduce heat to low and place a heatproof bowl over the saucepan and fill with chocolate, stirring, until completely melted.
5. Add the butter to the chocolate, and continue stirring, adding the cocoa powder until completely melted.

6. Whisk in the syrup, sugar, flour, vanilla, and salt.

7. Add the eggs and half of the chopped nuts and mix well.

8. Pour the mixture into the prepared shell and top with the remaining pecans.

9. Bake for 50-55 minutes

10. Allow cake to cool for about 4 hours

Nutrition:

960 Calories, 65g Fats, 13g Protein

My notes:

Peanut Butter Kisses

Preparation Time: 5 minutes
Cooking Time: 1 hour 20 minutes
Servings: 22

Ingredients:

- 1 ½ cups of smooth, unsweetened peanut butter
- 1 cup of coconut flour
- ¼ cup of keto sweetener (Swerve)
- a pinch of salt
- 1 tsp of vanilla extract
- 2 cups of dark chocolate
- 1 tbsp of coconut oil
- ¼ cup of nuts, chopped finely
- 4 tbsps. of peanut butter for drizzling

Directions:

1. Place the 1 ½ cups of peanut butter in a microwave safe dish and heat it for about 15 seconds to melt.
2. Pour the peanut butter, coconut flour, sweetener, vanilla extract, and salt in a medium bowl and mix until a smooth, thick paste is formed.
3. Prepare a baking tray and line it with parchment paper (make sure that this tray can fit in your freezer).
4. Use an ice cream scoop (preferably) to scoop the peanut butter mixture and place dollops of small circles of the mixture onto the baking tray (you should have about 20 scoops' worth). Place the tray in the freezer and allow the mixture to freeze for about 1 hour until firm.
5. When the peanut butter balls are almost ready, place the dark chocolate in a microwave safe bowl and microwave the chocolate until it has melted, then allow it to cool to room temperature.

6. Add the melted chocolate into a medium bowl, along with the coconut oil and the chopped nuts. Place the remaining 4 tbsps. of peanut butter into a microwave safe bowl and melt the peanut butter.
7. When the peanut butter balls are firm, use a fork to dip the balls into the chocolate mixture and place them back on the baking tray. Drizzle the peanut butter over the balls. Place the tray back into the freezer for another 10 minutes and enjoy cold.

Nutrition
259 Calories, 19g Carbohydrate, 18g Fats, 8g Protein

My notes:

Cornbread Muffins

Preparation Time: 10 minutes
Cooking Time: 25 minutes
Servings: 6-7

Ingredients:

- ½ cup butter softened
- ⅔ Cup white sugar
- ¼ cup honey
- Two eggs
- ½ teaspoon salt
- 1 ½ cups all-purpose flour
- ¾ cup cornmeal
- ½ teaspoon baking powder
- ½ cup milk
- ¾ cup frozen corn kernels, thawed

Directions:

1. Preheat oven to 400 grades F (200 grades C). Grease or 12 cups of muffins on deck.
2. Cream the butter, sugar, honey, eggs, and salt together in a big pot. Add in rice, cornmeal, and baking powder, blend well. Stir in corn and milk. Pour the yield into prepared muffin cups or spoon them.
3. Bake for 20 to 25 minutes in a preheated oven until a toothpick inserted in the center of a muffin comes out clean.

Nutrition:

141 Calories, 6g Protein, 22g Carbohydrate, 18g Fats

Chocolate Mousse Cake

Preparation Time: 10 minutes

Cooking Time: 25 minutes

Servings: 6-7

Ingredients:
- 1 (18.25 ounce) chocolate cake mix pack
- 1 (14 ounces) can sweeten condensed milk
- 2 (1 ounce) squares unsweetened chocolate, melted
- ½ cup of cold water
- 1 (3.9 ounces) package instant chocolate pudding mix
- 1 cup heavy cream, whipped

Directions:
1. Preheat oven up to 175 degrees C (350 degrees F). Prepare and bake cake mix on two 9-inch layers according to package Directions. Cool off and pan clean.
2. Mix the sweetened condensed milk and melted chocolate together in a big tub. Stir in water slowly, then pudding instantly until smooth. Chill in for 30 minutes, at least.
3. Remove from the fridge the chocolate mixture, and whisk to loosen. Fold in the whipped cream and head back to the refrigerator for at least another hour.

4. Place one of the cake layers onto a serving platter. Top the mousse with 1 1/2 cups, then cover with the remaining cake layer. Frost with remaining mousse, and cool until served. Garnish with chocolate shavings or fresh fruit.

Nutrition:

324 Calories, 8g Protein, 32g Carbohydrate, 50g Fats

My notes:

Blackberry and Apples Cobbler

Preparation Time: 10 minutes
Cooking Time: 30 minutes
Servings: 6

Ingredients:
- ¾ cup stevia
- 6 cups blackberries
- ¼ cup apples, cored and cubed
- ¼ teaspoon baking powder
- 1 tablespoon lime juice
- ½ cup almond flour
- ½ cup of water
- 3 and ½ tablespoon avocado oil
- Cooking spray

Directions:
1. In a bowl, mix the berries with half of the stevia and lemon juice, sprinkle some flour all over, whisk and pour into a baking dish greased with cooking spray.
2. In another bowl, mix flour with the rest of the sugar, baking powder, the water, and the oil, and stir the whole thing with your hands.
3. Spread over the berries, introduce in the oven at 375° F, and bake for 30 minutes. Serve warm.

My notes:

Nutrition:
221 Calories, 6.3g Fats,
6g Carbohydrates, 9g Protein

Delicious Ideas for Kids

Have you ever had the experience that you cooked for a long time and then your child did not want to eat?
Even their big guests are happy about lovingly prepared dishes.

Here are some suggestions:

Practical Advice for Beginners to Canning and Preserving your favorite Foods

There are a few safety tips that you should follow when you start canning and preserving foods from home. Canning is a great way to store and preserve foods, but it can be risky if not done correctly. However, if you follow these tips, you will be able to can foods safely.

Choose the Right Canner

The first step to safe home canning is choosing the right canner. First off, know when to use a pressure canner or a water bath canner.
Use a pressure canner that is specifically designed for canning and preserving foods. There are several types of canner out there, and some are just for cooking food, not for preserving food and processing jars. Be sure that you have the right type of equipment.

Make sure your pressure canner is the right size. If your canner is too small, the jars may be undercooked. Always opt for a larger canner as the pressure on the bigger pots tends to be more accurate, and you will be able to take advantage of the larger size and can more foods at once!

Before you begin canning, check that your pressure canner is in good condition. If your canner has a rubber gasket, it should be flexible and soft. If the rubber is dry or cracked, it should be replaced before you start canning. Be sure your canner is clean, and the small vents in the lid are free of debris. Adjust your canner for high altitude processing if needed.

Once you are sure your canner is ready to go and meets all these guidelines, it is time to start canning!

Opt for a Screw Top Lid System

There are many kinds of canning jars that you can choose to purchase. However, the only type of jar approved by the USDA is a mason jar with a screw-top lid. These are designated "preserving jars" and are considered the safest and most effective option for home preserving uses.

Some jars are not thought to be safe for home preservation despite being marketed as canning jars. Bail Jars, for example, have a two-part wire clasp lid with a rubber ring in between the lid and jar. While these were popular in the past, it is now thought that the thick rubber and tightly closed lid does not provide a sufficient seal, leading to a higher potential for botulism. Lightening Jars should not be used for canning as they are simply glass jars with glass lids, with no rubber at all. That will not create a good seal!

Reusing jars from store-bought products is another poor idea. They may look like they're in good condition, but they are typically designed to be processed in a commercial facility. Most store-bought products do not have the two-part band and lid system, which is best for home canning. The rubber seal on a store-bought product is likely not reusable once you open the original jar. You can reuse store-bought jars at home for storage but not for canning and preserving.

Check Your Jars, Lids, and Bands

As you wash your jars with soapy water, check for any imperfections. Even new jars may have a small chip or crack and need to be discarded. You can reuse jars again and again as long as they are in good condition.
The metal jar rings are also reusable; however, you should only reuse them if they are rust free and undented. If your bands begin to show signs of wear, consider investing in some new ones.

Jar lids need to be new as the sealing compound on the lid can disintegrate over time. When you store your jars in damp places (like in a basement or canning cellar), the lids are even more likely to disintegrate. Always use new lids to ensure that your canning is successful.

Check for Recent Canning Updates

Canning equipment has changed over the years, becoming higher-tech and, therefore, more efficient at processing foods. In addition to the equipment becoming more advanced, there have also been many scientific improvements, making canning safer when the proper steps are taken. For example, many people used to sterilize their jars before pressure canning. While this is still okay to do, it is unnecessary as science has shown that any bacteria in the jars will die when heated to such a high temperature in a pressure canner. Sterilization is an extra step that you don't need!
Make sure that your food preservation information is all up to date and uses current canning guidelines. Avoid outdated cookbooks and reassess "trusted family methods" to make sure they fit into the most recent criteria for safe canning. When in doubt, check with the US Department of Agriculture's Complete Guide to Home Canning, which contains the most recent, up-to-date canning tips.

Pick the Best Ingredients

When choosing food to can, always get the best food possible. You want to use high quality, perfectly ripe produce for canning. You will never end up with a jar of food better than the product itself, so picking good ingredients is important to your final product's taste. Also, products that past their prime can affect the ability to handle it. If strawberries are overripe, your jam may come out too runny. If your tomatoes are past their prime, they may not have a high enough pH level to be processed in a water bath. Pick your ingredients well, and you will make successfully preserved foods.

Clean everything

While you may know that your jars and lids need to be washed and sanitized, don't forget about the rest of your tools. Cleaning out your canner before using it is essential, even if you put it away clean. Make sure to wipe your countertop well, making sure there are no crumbs or residue. Wash your produce with clean, cold water, and don't forget to wash your hands! The cleaner everything is, the less likely you are to spread bacteria onto your jarred foods.

Follow Your Recipe

Use recipes from trusted sources, and be sure to follow them to the letter. Changing the amount of one or two ingredients may alter the balance of acidity and result in unsafe canning (especially when using a water bath canner). Use the ingredients as directed and make very few changes—none if possible.

Adhere to the processing times specified by your recipe. Sometimes the times may seem a little long, but the long processing time makes these products safe to store on the shelf. The processing time is the correct amount of time needed to destroy spoilage organisms, mold spores, yeast, and pathogens in the jar. So, as you may have guessed, it is extremely important to use the times written in your recipe as a hard rule.

Cool the Jars

Be sure that you give your jars 12 hours to cool before testing the seal. If you test the seal too early, it may break as the jar is still warm, making it pliable. Be sure to cool the jars away from a window or fan as even a slight breeze may cause the hot jars to crack. Once cool, remove the metal band, clean it and save it for your next canning project.

Conclusion

Dear Reader,

We're on the last few pages of this book, and I'd like to ask you how much you enjoyed flipping through it.

Did you find any new mouthwatering recipes?

Did you enjoy them on your own or with someone else?

And what did you think of the suggestions in the children's pages?

Maybe you've chosen from the index the recipes you've heard of before or those recipes that remind you of something you've already eaten with family and friends. Maybe you'll want to try all the recipes in this book.

... Take your time.

While you were reading, you probably also noticed how many and what dishes you can combine to surprise your guests, or maybe you found recipes that would taste better by changing a few ingredients and adding your personal touch.

Did you jot down your ideas in the notes section next to the recipes?

Have you noted in the tab below which page your favorite recipes are on?

Whether you're good in the kitchen or not, the recipes in this book are easy to prepare, don't require too many ingredients, and will allow you to recreate new masterworks every day that you, your family, and your guests will love.

A reason I sought out so-called "secret recipes" is the fact that once I found my favorite ones, I could enjoy them and combine them whenever I wanted to in the comfort of my own home.

Imagine being able to surprise your friends and family each time with the food they
most enjoyed at famous restaurants.

Imagine how satisfying it would be to show them that you created those masterworks in the comfort of your kitchen with these copycat recipes!

If you're in the mood for more tasty, easy-to-prepare recipes, contact your local bookseller and don't miss our upcoming cookbooks.

Also, by William Oliver Thomas & Ernest D.W.:

Copycat Dessert & Pastry Recipes for Beginners:
Discover how you can surprise your family and guests with these 50 easy, tasty, and low-cost recipes.

Copycat Recipes Beginner's guide:
Discover how you easily prepare delicious snacks, fresh fruit salads, and quenching soft drinks in a short time.

Copycat low-budget Cookbook for beginners:
Learn how to recreate and combine these 50 fast and tasty recipes in the comfort of your kitchen.

Beginners Guide to cooking Copycat Dishes:
How to satisfy with pleasure your five senses by preparing quickly and simply these 50 recipes.

Where are your sweetheart recipes?

Title   **Page**

CPSIA information can be obtained
at www.ICGtesting.com
Printed in the USA
BVHW090751030621
608729BV00002B/729